CELEBRATING HOLIDAYS

Labor Day

by Rachel Grack

BLASTOFF! READERS

BELLWETHER MEDIA • MINNEAPOLIS, MN

Note to Librarians, Teachers, and Parents:

Blastoff! Readers are carefully developed by literacy experts and combine standards-based content with developmentally appropriate text.

Level 1 provides the most support through repetition of high-frequency words, light text, predictable sentence patterns, and strong visual support.

Level 2 offers early readers a bit more challenge through varied simple sentences, increased text load, and less repetition of high-frequency words.

Level 3 advances early-fluent readers toward fluency through increased text and concept load, less reliance on visuals, longer sentences, and more literary language.

Level 4 builds reading stamina by providing more text per page, increased use of punctuation, greater variation in sentence patterns, and increasingly challenging vocabulary.

Level 5 encourages children to move from "learning to read" to "reading to learn" by providing even more text, varied writing styles, and less familiar topics.

Whichever book is right for your reader, Blastoff! Readers are the perfect books to build confidence and encourage a love of reading that will last a lifetime!

This edition first published in 2019 by Bellwether Media, Inc.

No part of this publication may be reproduced in whole or in part without written permission of the publisher. For information regarding permission, write to Bellwether Media, Inc., Attention: Permissions Department, 6012 Blue Circle Drive, Minnetonka, MN 55343.

Library of Congress Cataloging-in-Publication Data

Names: Koestler-Grack, Rachel A., 1973- author.
Title: Labor Day : by Rachel Grack.
Description: Minneapolis, MN : Bellwether Media, Inc., [2019] | Series: Blastoff! Readers: Celebrating Holidays | Includes bibliographical references and index. | Audience: Grades K-3. | Audience: Ages 5-8.
Identifiers: LCCN 2017056566 (print) | LCCN 2017056912 (ebook) | ISBN 9781626177895 (hardcover : alk. paper) | ISBN 9781681035185 (ebook)
Subjects: LCSH: Labor Day—Juvenile literature.
Classification: LCC HD7791 (ebook) | LCC HD7791 .K57 2018 (print) | DDC 394.264—dc23
LC record available at https://lccn.loc.gov/2017056566

Editor: Paige Polinsky · Designer: Andrea Schneider

Printed in the United States of America, North Mankato, MN.

Table of
Contents

Labor Day Is Here!

Families enjoy one last summer picnic. They wave flags as workers march in parades.

Later, fireworks light up the sky.
It is **Labor** Day!

What Is Labor Day?

Labor Day honors the **dignity** of United States workers. Their hard work helps America **prosper**.

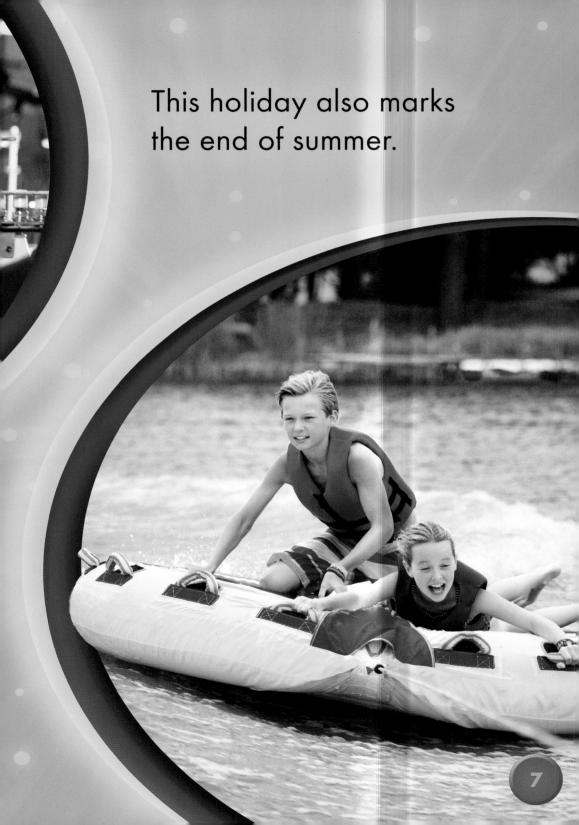

This holiday also marks the end of summer.

Who Celebrates Labor Day?

Americans and Canadians **observe** this holiday. Workers of all kinds celebrate with their friends and family.

St. Petersburg,
Russia

Other countries celebrate
workers on a different day.

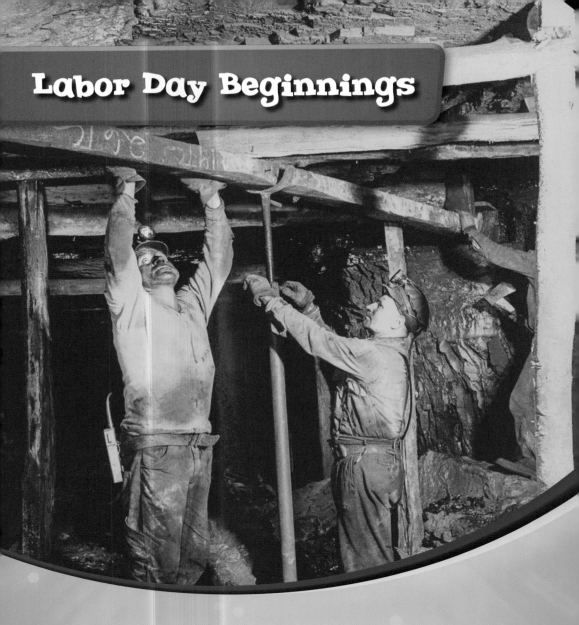

In the 1800s, American laborers were poorly paid. They worked long days with no time off.

Many held **strikes** and formed **labor unions**.

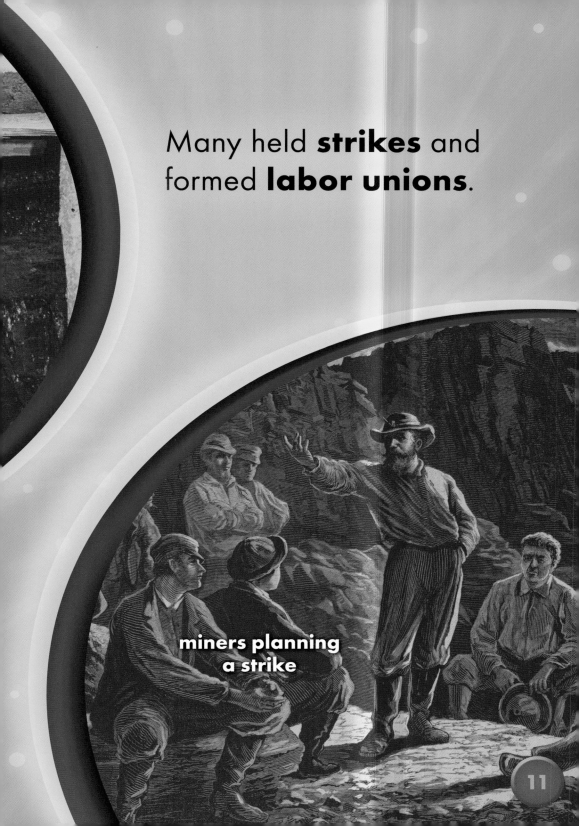

miners planning
a strike

In 1882, one union held a **festival** for workers. It took place in New York City on September 5.

This celebration **inspired** Labor Day.

Unions decided to celebrate workers every year.

Labor Day Timeline

1882 — First "workers' holiday" is celebrated in New York City

1884 — Unions pick the first Monday in September as Labor Day

1894 — Labor Day becomes a national holiday

They chose the first Monday in September as Labor Day. It became a **national** holiday in 1894.

Labor Day Traditions!

Many businesses close to give workers a day off. Some schools close, too. Cities hold colorful parades. Workers march together while crowds cheer.

Make a Handprint Flag

It takes the work of many hands to make America great. Show your respect for workers with this flag!

What You Need:

- scissors
- red and blue construction paper
- glue stick
- blue, red, and white craft paint
- paintbrushes
- white paint marker

What You Do:

1. Trim the blue paper so it is slightly smaller than the red. Glue it in the center of the red paper.
2. Paint a blue square on the bottom right corner of your left palm, across from your thumb.
3. Paint red and white stripes down the rest of your palm and fingers.
4. Press your painted hand on the center of the blue paper.
5. Let the paint dry. Then use the white marker to draw a star in the middle of the painted blue square.

3

4

Some people go to public
speeches on this day. They
learn about workers' **rights**.

Others celebrate the start of football season by going to games.

Many enjoy a long holiday weekend. Families take road trips and have barbecues.

They thank America's workers
with some end-of-summer fun!

Glossary

dignity—a way of behavior that calls for respect

festival—a celebration

inspired—caused something to happen or be created

labor—hard work

labor unions—groups of workers set up to help keep work safe and pay fair

national—related to the entire country

observe—to celebrate

prosper—to be successful

rights—things that the law says people can have or do, such as the right to fair pay

speeches—talks given to a group of people; on Labor Day, people might give speeches about workers' rights.

strikes—times when workers refuse to work until their needs are met

To Learn More

AT THE LIBRARY

Bowman, Chris. *Construction Workers*. Minneapolis, Minn.: Bellwether Media, 2018.

Dash, Meredith. *Labor Day*. Minneapolis, Minn.: Abdo Kids, 2015.

Grack, Rachel. *Veterans Day*. Minneapolis, Minn.: Bellwether Media, 2018.

ON THE WEB
Learning more about Labor Day is as easy as 1, 2, 3.

1. Go to www.factsurfer.com.

2. Enter "Labor Day" into the search box.

3. Click the "Surf" button and you will see a list of related web sites.

With factsurfer.com, finding more information is just a click away.

Index

The images in this book are reproduced through the courtesy of: Goodmorning3am, front cover; Olga Popova, front cover; rj lerich, front cover; Dragon Images, p. 4; Doug Lemke, pp. 4-5; michaeljung, pp. 6-7; YinYang, p. 7; wavebreakmedia, pp. 8, 16, 20-21; Roman Evgenev, pp. 8-9; John Collier/ wikicommons pp. 10-11; Science History Images/ Alamy, p. 11; Frank Leslie's Weekly Illustrated Newspaper/ wikicommons, p. 12; William Vandivert/ Getty Images, p. 14; Stockforlife, pp. 15, 22; Andrea Schneider/ Bellwether Media, p. 17 (all); Jim West/ Alamy, pp. 18-19; fitzcrittle, p. 19; alekleks, p. 20.